DO IT, Prompt Engineering

By: Dr. Joe G. Mucha, J.D.
       AI Prompt Doctor

This book is intended for informational purposes and should not be used as a substitute for professional advice and assistance. Please consult with a professional before making any decisions based on the information herein contained as the information contained in this book is based upon research and personal experience, but it is not guaranteed to be current, correct, and complete at the time of reading and as time moves forward. The authors and publishers of this book are not responsible for any errors or omissions, or for any actions taken based on the information provided. AI, ChatGPT and related technologies are constantly evolving, and the information contained herein, although current, correct, and accurate based upon knowledge, information, and belief, may not reflect the most current developments in this rapidly developing field.

Table of Contents

I.   The Future is Now: How AI NLP Prompt Engineering is Changing the World

AI NLP Prompt Engineering is rapidly transforming the way we live and work. As the field continues to advance, we can expect to see significant changes in various industries, from healthcare and finance to entertainment and education.

One of the key areas where AI NLP Prompt Engineering is making a difference is in natural language processing (NLP). With the help of machine learning algorithms and other AI technologies, NLP is becoming increasingly sophisticated, enabling machines to understand, interpret, and respond to human language in ways that were once impossible.

As a result, we are seeing a growing number of applications of NLP in our daily lives. From voice assistants like Siri and Alexa to chatbots that help us navigate customer service interactions, NLP is changing the way we interact with technology.

In the healthcare industry, NLP is helping medical professionals to better understand patient data and make more informed decisions. By analyzing patient records, lab results, and other sources of information, AI NLP Prompt Engineering is enabling doctors and nurses to diagnose illnesses more quickly and accurately, and to provide more personalized treatment plans.

In the finance industry, AI NLP Prompt Engineering is being used to analyze vast amounts of data and identify patterns that can be used to make more informed investment decisions. By processing news articles, social media posts, and other sources of information, AI NLP Prompt Engineering can help investors to stay ahead of trends and make better predictions about the markets.

The entertainment industry is also being transformed by AI NLP Prompt Engineering. From personalized recommendations on streaming platforms like Netflix and Amazon Prime to the creation of virtual assistants that can interact with users in real-time, NLP is enabling new forms of engagement and entertainment.

Healthcare: AI NLP Prompt Engineering is being used to analyze patient data and medical records, helping doctors and nurses to make more informed decisions about patient care. For example, NLP algorithms can analyze a patient's medical history, lab results, and other data to identify patterns and risk factors for certain conditions. This can help medical professionals to diagnose illnesses more quickly and accurately, and to develop more personalized treatment plans.

Finance: AI NLP Prompt Engineering is being used to analyze large amounts of financial data, helping investors to make more informed decisions about where to invest their money. For example, NLP algorithms can analyze news articles and social media posts to identify trends and sentiment around particular companies or industries. This information can then be used to make predictions about the markets and inform investment decisions.

Customer Service: AI NLP Prompt Engineering is being used to create chatbots and virtual assistants that can interact with customers in real-time. For example, a customer might interact with a chatbot to get help with a product or service. The chatbot uses NLP algorithms to understand the customer's request and provide a relevant response. This can help businesses to provide better customer service and improve customer satisfaction.

Entertainment: AI NLP Prompt Engineering is being used to personalize recommendations on streaming platforms like Netflix and Amazon Prime. For example, an NLP algorithm might analyze a user's viewing history and preferences to recommend other shows or movies that they might enjoy. This can help users to discover new content and stay engaged with the platform.

Marketing: AI NLP Prompt Engineering is being used to analyze customer feedback and sentiment on social media platforms. For example, an NLP algorithm might analyze Twitter or Facebook posts to understand what customers are saying about a particular brand or product. This information can then be used to improve marketing strategies and product development.

Education: AI NLP Prompt Engineering is being used to develop personalized learning experiences for students. For example, an NLP algorithm might analyze a student's performance on previous assignments to identify areas where they need more help. This information can then be used to develop a customized learning plan that meets the student's individual needs.

Human Resources: AI NLP Prompt Engineering is being used to screen job applicants and identify the most qualified candidates. For example, an NLP algorithm might analyze a candidate's resume and cover letter to identify keywords and skills that are relevant to the job opening. This information can then be used to narrow down the pool of candidates and identify the best fit for the position.

Social Services: AI NLP Prompt Engineering is being used to improve access to social services and support for vulnerable populations. For example, an NLP algorithm might analyze social media posts or other online data to identify individuals who may be at risk of homelessness or other forms of social exclusion. This information can then be used to connect these individuals with appropriate support services.

Legal: AI NLP Prompt Engineering is being used to automate legal document review and contract analysis. For example, an NLP algorithm might analyze a contract to identify key clauses and potential risks. This can help lawyers to save time and improve the accuracy of their work.

Transportation: AI NLP Prompt Engineering is being used to develop intelligent transportation systems that can improve traffic flow and reduce congestion. For example, an NLP algorithm might analyze traffic data and adjust traffic signals in real-time to optimize traffic flow.

E-commerce: AI NLP Prompt Engineering is being used to personalize online shopping experiences for customers. For example, an NLP algorithm might analyze a customer's browsing and purchasing history to recommend products that are relevant to their interests and preferences.

Journalism: AI NLP Prompt Engineering is being used to automate news article generation and analysis. For example, an NLP algorithm might analyze a large volume of news articles to identify key trends and topics.

Social Media: AI NLP Prompt Engineering is being used to identify fake news and other forms of misinformation on social media platforms. For example, an NLP algorithm might analyze the language and sources used in a news article to determine its credibility.

Energy: AI NLP Prompt Engineering is being used to optimize energy usage and reduce waste. For example, an NLP algorithm might analyze energy consumption data to identify patterns and inefficiencies that can be addressed.

Agriculture: AI NLP Prompt Engineering is being used to improve crop yields and reduce waste in agriculture. For example, an NLP algorithm might analyze weather data and soil conditions to determine the optimal time and conditions for planting and harvesting crops.

Gaming: AI NLP Prompt Engineering is being used to develop more immersive and interactive gaming experiences. For example, an NLP algorithm might analyze a player's speech and behavior to create a more personalized and engaging gaming experience.

Manufacturing: AI NLP Prompt Engineering is being used to optimize supply chain management and improve production efficiency. For example, an NLP algorithm might analyze production data to identify bottlenecks and other inefficiencies in the manufacturing process.

Government: AI NLP Prompt Engineering is being used to improve public services and engagement. For example, an NLP algorithm might analyze citizen feedback and sentiment to identify areas where government services can be improved.

As AI NLP Prompt Engineering continues to advance and become more integrated into various industries and sectors, we can expect to see a growing demand for professionals with the skills and knowledge to design, develop, and implement AI NLP Prompt Engineering solutions. This increased demand for skilled professionals is likely to lead to higher salaries for those with the requisite expertise.

According to data from the Bureau of Labor Statistics (BLS), the median annual wage for computer and information technology occupations, which includes many roles in AI NLP Prompt Engineering, was $91,250 as of May 2020. However, salaries can vary widely depending on factors such as education, experience, and job location.

As AI NLP Prompt Engineering continues to evolve and become more sophisticated, we can expect to see even higher salaries for those with specialized skills and experience. For example, professionals with a degree in AI NLP Prompt Engineering from a top-tier school like NLP Prompting Academy, combined with several years of experience in the field, may be able to command salaries in the range of $150,000 to $300,000 per year.

At the same time, entry-level positions in AI NLP Prompt Engineering, such as a Prompt Practitioner or Prompt Engineer, may offer starting salaries in the range of $70,000 to $100,000 per year. With experience and further education, these professionals can expect to earn higher salaries as they progress in their careers.

The salaries in AI NLP Prompt Engineering will depend on a variety of factors, including the level of education, work experience, and location. As the demand for skilled professionals in this field continues to grow, we can expect to see salaries trend upwards, making this an attractive career path for those looking to stay ahead of the curve in the exciting world of AI NLP Prompt Engineering.

The future of AI NLP Prompt Engineering is bright, and we can expect to see even more exciting developments in the years to come. As businesses and organizations continue to adopt these technologies, there will be a growing demand for professionals with the skills and knowledge to design and implement AI NLP Prompt Engineering solutions. Enrolling in a degree program at NLP Prompting Academy is an excellent way to get started on this career path and stay ahead of the curve in this exciting field.

Explanation of the Impact of AI NLP Prompt Engineering on Various Industries

AI NLP Prompt Engineering is having a profound impact on various industries, changing the way businesses operate and creating new opportunities for growth and innovation. Here are some examples of how AI NLP Prompt Engineering is affecting different industries:

Healthcare: AI NLP Prompt Engineering is transforming the healthcare industry by improving patient outcomes, reducing costs, and increasing efficiency. For example, AI NLP Prompt Engineering is being used to analyze patient data and medical records, helping doctors and nurses to make more informed decisions about patient care. This can lead to faster and more accurate diagnoses, more effective treatments, and better overall patient outcomes.

Finance: AI NLP Prompt Engineering is changing the finance industry by enabling better decision-making, improving risk management, and increasing efficiency. For example, AI NLP Prompt Engineering is being used to analyze large amounts of financial data, helping investors to make more informed decisions about where to invest their money. This can lead to better investment outcomes and reduced risk for investors.

Customer Service: AI NLP Prompt Engineering is transforming the customer service industry by improving response times, reducing costs, and increasing customer satisfaction. For example, AI NLP Prompt Engineering is being used to create chatbots and virtual assistants that can interact with customers in real-time, helping to answer questions and resolve issues quickly and efficiently.

Marketing: AI NLP Prompt Engineering is changing the marketing industry by enabling more targeted and personalized marketing campaigns. For example, AI NLP Prompt Engineering is being used to analyze customer feedback and sentiment on social media platforms, helping marketers to better understand their customers and develop more effective marketing strategies.

Education: AI NLP Prompt Engineering is transforming the education industry by enabling more personalized and effective learning experiences. For example, AI NLP Prompt Engineering is being used to develop customized learning plans for students, helping them to learn at their own pace and in a way that best fits their individual needs.

Entertainment: AI NLP Prompt Engineering is changing the entertainment industry by enabling more personalized and engaging experiences for users. For example, AI NLP Prompt Engineering is being used to personalize recommendations on streaming platforms like Netflix and Amazon Prime, helping users to discover new content and stay engaged with the platform.

Transportation: AI NLP Prompt Engineering is transforming the transportation industry by improving safety, reducing congestion, and increasing efficiency. For example, AI NLP Prompt Engineering is being used to develop intelligent transportation systems that can optimize traffic flow and reduce congestion on busy roads.

As AI NLP Prompt Engineering continues to evolve and become more sophisticated, there will be an increasing need for individuals with the skills and knowledge to design, develop, and implement AI NLP Prompt Engineering solutions in various industries.

According to a report by the World Economic Forum, AI and machine learning technologies are expected to create 133 million new jobs globally by 2022. While this figure includes a wide range of jobs in the field of AI, it's clear that there will be significant demand for professionals with skills in areas like NLP and prompt engineering.

Additionally, as AI NLP Prompt Engineering becomes more integrated into various industries and sectors, there will be a growing demand for professionals with specialized skills and expertise in these areas. This includes individuals with degrees in AI NLP Prompt Engineering from top-tier schools like the NLP Prompting Academy, who will be well-positioned to take on leadership roles in the development and implementation of AI NLP Prompt Engineering solutions.

As demand for skilled professionals in Prompt Engineering continuesto grow, we can expect to see increasing wages for those with the requisite expertise. According to data from the Bureau of Labor Statistics (BLS), the median annual wage for computer and information technology occupations, which includes many roles in AI NLP Prompt Engineering, was $91,250 as of May 2020. However, as demand for skilled professionals in this field increases, we can expect to see higher salaries for those with specialized skills and experience, ranging from $70,000 to $300,000 per year. It's clear that there will be significant demand for skilled professionals in this field, with opportunities for high-paying careers for those with the requisite skills and expertise. Enrolling in a degree program at NLP Prompting Academy can help individuals to develop these skills and prepare for a rewarding career in this exciting and rapidly growing field.

AI NLP Prompt Engineering is having a profound impact on various industries, enabling businesses to operate more efficiently, make better decisions, and provide better experiences for their customers. As AI NLP Prompt Engineering continues to evolve and become more sophisticated, we can expect to see even more exciting developments in the years to come.

Overview of the growing demand for professionals with AI NLP Prompt Engineering skills

The demand for professionals with AI NLP Prompt Engineering skills is growing rapidly, driven by the increasing adoption of AI and machine learning technologies in various industries and sectors. As AI NLP Prompt Engineering becomes more integrated into business operations, there is a growing need for individuals with the skills and knowledge to design, develop, and implement AI NLP Prompt Engineering solutions.

According to a report by the World Economic Forum, AI and machine learning technologies are expected to create 133 million new jobs globally by 2022. While this figure includes a wide range of jobs in the field of AI, it's clear that there will be significant demand for professionals with skills in areas like NLP and prompt engineering.

As businesses and organizations continue to adopt AI NLP Prompt Engineering solutions, there will be a growing demand for professionals with specialized skills and expertise in these areas. This includes individuals with degrees in AI NLP Prompt Engineering from top-tier schools like the NLP Prompting Academy, who will be well-positioned to take on leadership roles in the development and implementation of AI NLP Prompt Engineering solutions.

Enrolling in a degree program at NLP Prompting Academy can help individuals to develop the skills and knowledge needed to succeed in this exciting and rapidly growing field. The Academy offers a comprehensive curriculum that covers a wide range of topics in AI NLP Prompt Engineering, including natural language processing, machine learning, data science, and more. Students have the opportunity to work with experienced faculty members and industry professionals, gaining hands-on experience in developing AI NLP Prompt Engineering solutions.

In addition to providing a comprehensive education in AI NLP Prompt Engineering, the NLP Prompting Academy offers a range of resources and support services to help students succeed. This includes career services, networking opportunities, and access to cutting-edge research and development in the field.

Enrolling in a degree program at NLP Prompting Academy can help individuals to develop the skills and knowledge needed to succeed in the growing field of AI NLP Prompt Engineering. With demand for skilled professionals in this field on the rise, now is the perfect time to invest in your education and prepare for a rewarding career in this exciting and rapidly evolving field.

II. Meet NLP Prompting Academy: Your Gateway to AI NLP Prompt Engineering Education

NLP Prompting Academy is a leading institution that provides world-class education in the field of AI NLP Prompt Engineering. Our mission is to equip students with the skills and knowledge they need to succeed in this exciting and rapidly growing field, and to help them become leaders in the development and implementation of AI NLP Prompt Engineering solutions.

At NLP Prompting Academy, we offer a comprehensive curriculum that covers a wide range of topics in AI NLP Prompt Engineering, including natural language processing, machine learning, data science, and more. Our faculty members are experienced professionals with years of experience in the field, and they are committed to providing students with the support and guidance they need to succeed.

In addition to our comprehensive curriculum, we offer a range of resources and support services to help students succeed. This includes career services, networking opportunities, and access to cutting-edge research and development in the field. Our students also have the opportunity to work on real-world projects, gaining hands-on experience in developing AI NLP Prompt Engineering solutions that have real-world impact.

One of the unique aspects of NLP Prompting Academy is our commitment to providing a personalized and flexible learning experience. We understand that every student has their own learning style and pace, which is why we offer a range of flexible learning options, including online courses and part-time programs. This allows students to balance their education with other commitments, while still getting the comprehensive education and support they need to succeed.

At NLP Prompting Academy, we believe that education should be accessible to everyone. That's why we offer a range of financial aid and scholarship opportunities to help make our programs more affordable for students from all backgrounds. We also have a diverse and inclusive community, welcoming students from all over the world and from a wide range of backgrounds and experiences.

The NLP Prompting Academy is your gateway to AI NLP Prompt Engineering education. Whether you're just starting out in your career or looking to take your skills to the next level, our comprehensive curriculum, experienced faculty, and flexible learning options can help you achieve your goals and succeed in this exciting and rapidly growing field.

Introduction to NLP Prompting Academy and its Mission.

The NLP Prompting Academy is at the forefront of the new AI revolution, providing cutting-edge education and training in AI NLP Prompt Engineering to help students survive, thrive, and profit from the rapid changes happening in the industry. Our mission is to provide students with the knowledge, skills, and resources they need to succeed in this exciting and rapidly evolving field.

At NLP Prompting Academy, we recognize that AI NLP Prompt Engineering is one of the fastest-growing and most exciting areas of technology, and that there is a significant demand for professionals with specialized skills and expertise in this field. Our programs are designed to meet this demand, providing students with a comprehensive education in AI NLP Prompt Engineering that covers a wide range of topics, including natural language processing, machine learning, data science, and more.

One of the unique aspects of NLP Prompting Academy is our commitment to staying at the forefront of the industry. We believe that education is not just about teaching students what is happening now, but also about preparing them for the future. That's why our faculty members are experienced professionals with years of experience in the field, and why we invest heavily in research and development to ensure that our curriculum is always up-to-date and relevant.

In addition to providing a comprehensive education in AI NLP Prompt Engineering, we are also committed to creating a dialogue about the role of technology in society. We believe that it is important to consider not just the technological advancements themselves, but also the social, ethical, and political implications of these advancements. Through our programs and events, we encourage students to engage in meaningful discussions about these issues, and to think critically about the impact of AI NLP Prompt Engineering on society as a whole.

The NLP Prompting Academy is an institution that is dedicated to helping students survive, thrive, and profit from the new AI revolution. Our mission is to provide students with a comprehensive education in AI NLP Prompt Engineering, and to create a dialogue about the role of technology in society. We believe that by investing in education and training in this exciting and rapidly growing field, we can help individuals to achieve their goals and contribute to the advancement of society as a whole.

Overview of the Degree Programs Offered at the School

At NLP Prompting Academy, we offer four-degree programs in AI NLP Prompt Engineering: Prompt Practitioner, Prompt Engineer, Prompt Master, and Prompt Doctor. These programs are designed to provide students with a comprehensive education in AI NLP Prompt Engineering, with a focus on developing the skills and expertise needed to succeed in various roles and industries.

The Prompt Practitioner program is an introductory program that covers the basics of AI NLP Prompt Engineering, including natural language processing, machine learning, and data science. This program is designed for individuals who are new to the field and want to gain a foundational understanding of the concepts and tools used in AI NLP Prompt Engineering.

The Prompt Engineer program is a more advanced program that builds on the concepts covered in the Prompt Practitioner program. This program covers a wider range of topics, including deep learning, computer vision, and robotics, and is designed for individuals who want to take their skills to the next level and work in more specialized roles in the field.

The Prompt Master program is a graduate-level program that provides students with advanced training in AI NLP Prompt Engineering. This program is designed for individuals who want to become leaders in the field and work on cutting-edge research and development projects. Students in this program have the opportunity to work on research projects in collaboration with faculty members and industry partners.

The Prompt Doctor program is a doctoral-level program that focuses on advanced research in AI NLP Prompt Engineering. This program is designed for individuals who want to make significant contributions to the field through research and development of new technologies and solutions.

The degree programs offered at NLP Prompting Academy provide students with a comprehensive education in AI NLP Prompt Engineering, with a focus on developing the skills and expertise needed to succeed in various roles and industries. Our experienced faculty members, cutting-edge research, and personalized learning approach ensure that students receive the highest quality education and training in this exciting and rapidly growing field.

Salaries for individuals with degrees in AI NLP Prompt Engineering from NLP Prompting Academy can vary depending on a variety of factors, including experience, location, and industry. However, in general, individuals with these degrees can expect to earn competitive salaries in the field.

According to data from the Bureau of Labor Statistics (BLS), the median annual wage for computer and information technology occupations, which includes many roles in AI NLP Prompt Engineering, was $91,250 as of May 2020. However, as demand for skilled professionals in this field increases, we can expect to see higher salaries for those with specialized skills and experience, ranging from $70,000 to $300,000 per year.

Individuals with a degree in Prompt Practitioner can expect to earn an entry-level salary of around $70,000 to $80,000 per year. Those with a degree in Prompt Engineer can earn a salary of around $90,000 to $120,000 per year. Individuals with a degree in Prompt Master can earn a salary of around $120,000 to $180,000 per year, while those with a degree in Prompt Doctor can expect to earn even higher salaries, up to $300,000 per year.

It's important to note that salaries can vary significantly depending on factors such as location and industry. For example, salaries for AI NLP Prompt Engineering professionals in technology hubs like Silicon Valley or New York City may be higher than those in other parts of the country. Additionally, individuals working in industries like finance or healthcare may earn higher salaries than those working in other sectors.

Overall, individuals with degrees in AI NLP Prompt Engineering from NLP Prompting Academy can expect to earn competitive salaries in this exciting and rapidly growing field. With opportunities for high-paying careers and a growing demand for skilled professionals in this field, now is the perfect time to invest in your education and prepare for a rewarding career in AI NLP Prompt Engineering.

III.　The Four Degrees of Prompt Engineering: Which One is Right for You

At NLP Prompting Academy, we offer four degrees in AI NLP Prompt Engineering: Prompt Practitioner, Prompt Engineer, Prompt Master, and Prompt Doctor. Each degree program is designed to provide students with a comprehensive education in AI NLP Prompt Engineering, with a focus on developing the skills and expertise needed to succeed in various roles and industries.

The Prompt Practitioner degree program is an introductory program that covers the basics of AI NLP Prompt Engineering. This program is designed for individuals who are new to the field and want to gain a foundational understanding of the concepts and tools used in AI NLP Prompt Engineering. The program covers topics like natural language processing, machine learning, and data science.

The Prompt Engineer degree program is a more advanced program that builds on the concepts covered in the Prompt Practitioner program. This program covers a wider range of topics, including deep learning, computer vision, and robotics. It is designed for individuals who want to take their skills to the next level and work in more specialized roles in the field.

The Prompt Master degree program is a graduate-level program that provides students with advanced training in AI NLP Prompt Engineering. This program is designed for individuals who want to become leaders in the field and work on cutting-edge research and development projects. Students in this program have the opportunity to work on research projects in collaboration with faculty members and industry partners.

The Prompt Doctor degree program is a doctoral-level program that focuses on advanced research in AI NLP Prompt Engineering. This program is designed for individuals who want to make significant contributions to the field through research and development of new technologies and solutions.

When considering which degree program is right for you, it's important to consider your goals and career aspirations. If you're new to the field and want to gain a foundational understanding of AI NLP Prompt Engineering, the Prompt Practitioner degree program may be the best option. If you want to take your skills to the next level and work in specialized roles, the Prompt Engineer degree program may be the right choice.

If you're interested in becoming a leader in the field and working on cutting-edge research and development projects, the Prompt Master degree program may be the best option. And if you want to make significant contributions to the field through advanced research, the Prompt Doctor degree program may be the ideal choice.

Each degree program offered at NLP Prompting Academy is designed to meet the needs of individuals with different goals and aspirations in the field of AI NLP Prompt Engineering. By carefully considering your career goals and choosing the right degree program, you can gain the skills and expertise needed to succeed in this exciting and rapidly evolving field.

Detailed Description of Each Degree Program, Including Coursework and Career Prospects

At NLP Prompting Academy, we offer four-degree programs in AI NLP Prompt Engineering: Prompt Practitioner, Prompt Engineer, Prompt Master, and Prompt Doctor. Each degree program is designed to provide students with a comprehensive education in AI NLP Prompt Engineering, with a focus on developing the skills and expertise needed to succeed in various roles and industries. Here is a detailed description of each degree program:

Prompt Practitioner:
The Prompt Practitioner degree program is an introductory program that covers the basics of AI NLP Prompt Engineering. This program is designed for individuals who are new to the field and want to gain a foundational understanding of the concepts and tools used in AI NLP Prompt

Engineering. Coursework includes topics like natural language processing, machine learning, data science, and more. Career prospects for individuals with a degree in Prompt Practitioner include roles like data analyst, business analyst, and entry-level machine learning engineer.

Prompt Engineer:
The Prompt Engineer degree program is a more advanced program that builds on the concepts covered in the Prompt Practitioner program. This program covers a wider range of topics, including deep learning, computer vision, and robotics. It is designed for individuals who want to take their skills to the next level and work in more specialized roles in the field. Coursework includes advanced topics in AI NLP Prompt Engineering and practical applications of the concepts learned. Career prospects for individuals with a degree in Prompt Engineer include roles like machine learning engineer, software engineer, and AI developer.

Prompt Master:

The Prompt Master's degree program is a graduate-level program that provides students with advanced training in AI NLP Prompt Engineering. This program is designed for individuals who want to become leaders in the field and work on cutting-edge research and development projects. Coursework includes advanced topics in AI NLP Prompt Engineering, research methods, and practical applications of the concepts learned. Career prospects for individuals with a degree in Prompt Master include roles like research scientist, data scientist, and AI researcher.

Prompt Doctor:

The Prompt Doctor degree program is a doctoral-level program that focuses on advanced research in AI NLP Prompt Engineering. This program is designed for individuals who want to make significant contributions to the field through research and development of new technologies and solutions. Coursework includes advanced research methods, specialized topics in AI NLP Prompt Engineering, and a dissertation.

Career prospects for individuals with a degree in Prompt Doctor include roles like chief technology officer, research director, and AI strategist.

Each degree program offered at NLP Prompting Academy is designed to provide students with a comprehensive education in AI NLP Prompt Engineering, with a focus on developing the skills and expertise needed to succeed in various roles and industries. By carefully considering your career goals and choosing the right degree program, you can gain the skills and expertise needed to succeed in this exciting and rapidly evolving field.

At NLP Prompting Academy, we offer four-degree programs in AI NLP Prompt Engineering: Prompt Practitioner, Prompt Engineer, Prompt Master, and Prompt Doctor. Each degree program provides students with a comprehensive education in AI NLP Prompt Engineering and offers unique career and salary prospects. Here is an overview of the career and salary prospects for each degree:

Prompt Practitioner:
Individuals with a degree in Prompt Practitioner can expect to earn an entry-level salary of around $70,000 to $80,000 per year. Career prospects for individuals with a degree in Prompt Practitioner include roles like data analyst, business analyst, and entry-level machine learning engineer. These professionals work with data to develop insights, solve problems, and develop algorithms. With the growing demand for data-driven decision making in various industries, the job prospects for Prompt Practitioner degree holders are expected to remain strong.

Prompt Engineer:
Individuals with a degree in Prompt Engineer can earn a salary of around $90,000 to $120,000 per year. Career prospects for individuals with a degree in Prompt Engineer include roles like machine learning engineer,

48

software engineer, and AI developer. These professionals work on designing, developing, and implementing AI systems and solutions. As AI becomes more integrated into various industries, the demand for Prompt Engineer degree holders is expected to increase.

Prompt Master:
Individuals with a degree in Prompt Master can earn a salary of around $120,000 to $180,000 per year. Career prospects for individuals with a degree in Prompt Master include roles like research scientist, data scientist, and AI researcher. These professionals work on developing new AI systems, technologies, and solutions. With the increasing demand for AI-driven innovation and development, the job prospects for Prompt master's degree holders are expected to remain strong.

Prompt Doctor:
Individuals with a degree in Prompt Doctor can expect to earn even higher salaries, up to $300,000 per year. Career prospects for individuals with a degree in Prompt Doctor

include roles like chief technology officer, research director, and AI strategist. These professionals work on developing cutting-edge AI solutions, leading research projects, and making strategic decisions related to AI. As AI becomes more integrated into various industries, the demand for Prompt Doctor degree holders is expected to increase.

Each degree program offered at NLP Prompting Academy provides students with a comprehensive education in AI NLP Prompt Engineering and offers promising career and salary prospects. With the increasing demand for AI-driven solutions and the growing role of AI in various industries, pursuing a degree in AI NLP Prompt Engineering from NLP Prompting Academy can be a smart choice for individuals who want to succeed in this exciting and rapidly growing field.

Comparison of the Degree Programs to Help You Choose the Best Fit for Your Goals

When it comes to choosing a degree program in AI NLP Prompt Engineering, it's important to consider your goals, time commitment, and desired salary. NLP Prompting Academy offers four-degree programs in AI NLP Prompt Engineering: Prompt Practitioner, Prompt Engineer, Prompt Master, and Prompt Doctor. Here is a comparison of the degree programs to help you choose the best fit for your goals:

Time Commitment:
The Prompt Practitioner program is the shortest program and can be completed in around 9-12 months. The Prompt Engineer program is a more advanced program that typically takes around 12-18 months to complete. The Prompt Master program is a graduate-level program that typically takes around 18-24 months to complete. The Prompt Doctor program is a doctoral-level program that typically takes around 3-5 years

to complete or less depending on ability, determination and talent.

Desired Salary:
Individuals with a degree in Prompt Practitioner can expect to earn an entry-level salary of around $70,000 to $80,000 per year. Individuals with a degree in Prompt Engineer can earn a salary of around $90,000 to $120,000 per year. Individuals with a degree in Prompt Master can earn a salary of around $120,000 to $180,000 per year. Individuals with a degree in Prompt Doctor can expect to earn even higher salaries, up to $300,000 per year.

Perseverance:
The Prompt Practitioner program is an introductory program that covers the basics of AI NLP Prompt Engineering. It is a good fit for individuals who want to gain a foundational understanding of the concepts and tools used in AI NLP Prompt Engineering. The Prompt Engineer program is a more advanced program that is a good fit for individuals who want to take their skills

to the next level and work in more specialized roles in the field. The Prompt Master program is a graduate-level program that is a good fit for individuals who want to become leaders in the field and work on cutting-edge research and development projects. The Prompt Doctor program is a doctoral-level program that is a good fit for individuals who want to make significant contributions to the field through research and development of new technologies and solutions.

Choosing the best degree program in AI NLP Prompt Engineering depends on your goals, time commitment, and desired salary. By considering these factors and carefully evaluating each degree program, you can choose the best fit for your needs and prepare for a successful career in this exciting and rapidly growing field.

IV. Learning in the Digital Age: Advantages of Online Learning at NLP Prompting Academy

Online learning has become increasingly popular in recent years, and for good reasons. The advantages of online learning in the digital age are numerous, especially when it comes to learning AI NLP Prompt Engineering at NLP Engineering Academy.

Flexibility:
One of the most significant advantages of online learning is flexibility. Online learning allows students to study at their own pace and on their own schedule, which is especially useful for those who have work or other commitments. At NLP Engineering Academy, students can access course materials and assignments from anywhere with an internet connection, making it easy to learn on-the-go.

Access to Expertise:
Another advantage of online learning is the access to expertise. At NLP Engineering Academy, we have a team of experienced faculty members who are experts in AI NLP Prompt Engineering. With online learning, students have access to these experts from anywhere in the world. This provides an opportunity to learn from the best and receive personalized guidance and feedback.

Interactive Learning:
Online learning also offers interactive learning experiences that can enhance the learning process. At NLP Engineering Academy, students can participate in live online classes and interact with their peers and instructors in real-time. Additionally, our online platform offers discussion boards and group projects that encourage collaboration and a sense of community among students.

Cost-Effective:
Online learning can also be cost-effective, as it eliminates the need for expenses like

transportation, housing, and other related costs. At NLP Engineering Academy, we offer our programs at a competitive price point, making it accessible for individuals who want to upskill or enter the field of AI NLP Prompt Engineering.

Self-Paced Learning:
Online learning allows for self-paced learning, which can be particularly beneficial for those who learn at different speeds or have different learning styles. At NLP Engineering Academy, students can progress through their coursework at their own pace, which can help to ensure a more thorough understanding of the material.

Innovative Technology:
Online learning also allows for the use of innovative technology in the classroom. At NLP Engineering Academy, we use the latest tools and technologies to deliver high-quality instruction and provide students with hands-on experience in AI NLP Prompt Engineering.

Global Community:
Online learning can also provide access to a global community of learners. At NLP Engineering Academy, our online platform allows students from all over the world to connect and collaborate, which can broaden perspectives and provide a more diverse learning experience.

Continued Support:
Online learning also offers continued support for students. At NLP Engineering Academy, we offer ongoing support through our online platform, which includes access to course materials, discussion forums, and one-on-one support from faculty members.

Higher Earning Potential:
Online learning can lead to higher earning potential in the field of AI NLP Prompt Engineering. According to data from Glassdoor, the median salary for a machine learning engineer in the US is over $114,000 per year. By pursuing a degree in AI NLP Prompt Engineering at NLP Engineering

Academy, students can gain the skills and expertise needed to succeed in this lucrative field and earn from $70,000 to $300,000 per year.

Career Advancement:
Online learning can also help individuals advance their careers in AI NLP Prompt Engineering. At NLP Engineering Academy, we offer four-degree programs in AI NLP Prompt Engineering, ranging from the introductory level to the doctoral level. By pursuing a degree in AI NLP Prompt Engineering, individuals can gain the skills and expertise needed to take on more advanced roles in the field, which can lead to increased earning potential and career advancement.

Convenient and Accessible:
Online learning is also convenient and accessible. At NLP Engineering Academy, our online platform allows students to access course materials and assignments from anywhere with an internet connection. This makes it easy to learn on-the-go and to

balance coursework with other commitments, such as work or family.

Affordable:
Online learning can also be affordable. At NLP Engineering Academy, we offer our programs at a competitive price point, making it accessible for individuals who want to upskill or enter the field of AI NLP Prompt Engineering without incurring significant debt.

Online learning offers numerous advantages when it comes to learning AI NLP Prompt Engineering at NLP Engineering Academy. With flexibility, access to expertise, interactive learning experiences, and cost-effectiveness, online learning is a great option for individuals who want to advance their education and career in this exciting and rapidly growing field.

Overview of The Benefits of Online Learning, Including Flexibility, Accessibility, and Cost-Effectiveness

Online learning has become increasingly popular in recent years, and for good reasons. There are numerous benefits of online learning, especially when it comes to learning AI NLP Prompt Engineering at NLP Engineering Academy. Here is an overview of the benefits of online learning:

Flexibility:
One of the most significant benefits of online learning is flexibility. Online learning allows students to study at their own pace and on their own schedule, which is especially useful for those who have work or other commitments. At NLP Engineering Academy, students can access course materials and assignments from anywhere with an internet connection, making it easy to learn on-the-go.

Accessibility:
Online learning is also accessible. With online learning, students can access high-quality education from anywhere in the world, without the need to relocate or commute. This makes education more accessible to individuals who may not have had the opportunity to pursue a degree in AI NLP Prompt Engineering otherwise.

Cost-Effectiveness:
Online learning can also be cost-effective. Online learning eliminates the need for expenses like transportation, housing, and other related costs. Additionally, at NLP Engineering Academy, we offer our programs at a competitive price point, making it accessible for individuals who want to upskill or enter the field of AI NLP Prompt Engineering without incurring significant debt.

Interactive Learning:
Online learning also offers interactive learning experiences that can enhance the learning process. At NLP Engineering Academy, students can participate in live online classes and interact with their peers and instructors in real-time. Additionally, our online platform offers discussion boards and group projects that encourage collaboration and a sense of community among students.

Expertise:
Online learning also provides access to expertise. At NLP Engineering Academy, we have a team of experienced faculty members who are experts in AI NLP Prompt Engineering. With online learning, students have access to these experts from anywhere in the world, which provides an opportunity to learn from the best and receive personalized guidance and feedback.

Online learning provides numerous benefits when it comes to learning AI NLP Prompt Engineering at NLP Engineering Academy. With flexibility, accessibility, cost-effectiveness, interactive learning experiences, and access to expertise, online learning is a great option for individuals who want to advance their education and career in this exciting and rapidly growing field.

Discussion of NLP Prompting Academy's Online Learning Environment, Resources, and Support Services

NLP Engineering Academy offers a robust online learning environment that provides students with access to a wide range of resources and support services. Here is a discussion of the online learning environment, resources, and support services available at NLP Engineering Academy:

Online Learning Environment:
NLP Engineering Academy's online learning environment is designed to provide students with a comprehensive and engaging learning experience. Our platform offers an intuitive interface that is easy to navigate, and it provides access to course materials, assignments, and online lectures. Additionally, our platform offers discussion boards, chat rooms, and other interactive tools that encourage collaboration and community-building among students.

Resources:

NLP Engineering Academy provides students with access to a wide range of resources to support their learning. Our platform offers a variety of multimedia resources, including videos, articles, and case studies, that provide real-world examples of the concepts and tools used in AI NLP Prompt Engineering. Additionally, our platform offers online tutorials, study guides, and other materials that help students master the material covered in their courses.

Support Services:
NLP Engineering Academy offers a variety of support services to help students succeed in their coursework. Our faculty members are experienced experts in AI NLP Prompt Engineering and are available to provide students with one-on-one guidance and feedback. Additionally, our platform offers technical support to ensure that students can access course materials and assignments without any issues. Our platform also offers career services, including resume reviews and interview coaching, to help students prepare for success in the job market.

The NLP Engineering Academy provides students with a comprehensive online learning environment that is designed to support their learning and success. With a wide range of resources and support services, students can access the tools and expertise they need to advance their education and career in AI NLP Prompt Engineering.

V. The NLP Engineering Academy Learning Experience: What to Expect

The NLP Engineering Academy offers a unique and comprehensive learning experience for individuals who want to gain expertise in AI NLP Prompt Engineering. Here is what students can expect when they enroll in our programs:

In-Depth Coursework:
Our degree programs in AI NLP Prompt Engineering are designed to provide students with a deep understanding of the concepts and tools used in this exciting and rapidly growing field. Our coursework is designed to be rigorous and challenging, but also accessible and engaging. Students can expect to cover topics such as natural language processing, machine learning, data analytics, and more.

Expert Faculty:
At NLP Engineering Academy, our faculty members are experts in AI NLP Prompt Engineering and have extensive experience

working in the field. Our faculty members are dedicated to providing students with a high-quality education that prepares them for success in their careers. Students can expect to receive personalized guidance and feedback from our faculty members throughout their coursework.

Interactive Learning:
Our online learning platform is designed to provide students with an interactive and engaging learning experience. Students can participate in live online classes, interact with their peers and instructors in real-time, and collaborate on group projects and assignments. Our platform also offers discussion boards and chat rooms that allow students to connect with each other and build a sense of community.

Flexible Learning:
At NLP Engineering Academy, we understand that our students have busy schedules and other commitments. That's why our online learning platform is designed to be flexible and accessible. Students can

access course materials and assignments from anywhere with an internet connection and can progress through their coursework at their own pace.

Career Services:
At NLP Engineering Academy, we are committed to helping our students succeed in their careers. That's why we offer a range of career services, including resume reviews and interview coaching. We also provide students with access to a network of alumni and industry professionals, which can help to open doors to exciting job opportunities.

The NLP Engineering Academy learning experience is designed to provide students with a comprehensive and engaging education in AI NLP Prompt Engineering. With in-depth coursework, expert faculty, interactive learning, flexible scheduling, and career services, students can expect to gain the skills and expertise needed to succeed in this exciting and rapidly growing field.

Overview of The School's Teaching Philosophy and Methods

At NLP Engineering Academy, we believe in a teaching philosophy that is centered around student success and engagement. Here is an overview of our teaching philosophy and methods:

Active Learning:
We believe that active learning is the key to effective education. Our coursework is designed to be interactive and engaging, with opportunities for students to participate in group projects, discussions, and other activities that allow them to apply their knowledge in real-world settings. By actively engaging with the material, students can deepen their understanding and develop the critical thinking skills needed to succeed in AI NLP Prompt Engineering.

Experienced Faculty:
Our faculty members are experienced experts in AI NLP Prompt Engineering and are dedicated to providing students with a high-

quality education. Our faculty members are accessible and supportive and are committed to helping students succeed in their coursework and careers. We believe that our faculty members' expertise and experience are critical components of our teaching philosophy and methods.

Technology-Driven:
We believe that technology can be a powerful tool for education. At NLP Engineering Academy, we use the latest tools and technologies to deliver high-quality instruction and provide students with hands-on experience in AI NLP Prompt Engineering. Our online learning platform is designed to be interactive and user-friendly, with multimedia resources and other tools that enhance the learning experience.

Student-Centered:
We believe that students should be at the center of their education. Our coursework is designed to be flexible and accessible, with students able to progress through their coursework at their own pace. Our faculty

members provide personalized guidance and feedback to help students succeed in their coursework and careers.

Hands-On Learning:
We believe that hands-on learning is essential to effective education. At NLP Engineering Academy, we provide students with opportunities to apply their knowledge in real-world settings, such as through internships, capstone projects, and other experiential learning opportunities. By engaging with the material in practical settings, students can develop the skills and experience needed to succeed in AI NLP Prompt Engineering.

Collaborative Learning:
We believe that learning is a collaborative process. Our coursework is designed to encourage collaboration and community-building among students. Our online learning platform offers discussion boards, chat rooms, and other tools that allow students to connect with each other and with their instructors. By working together, students

can learn from each other's perspectives and experiences, and can develop important teamwork skills.

Continuous Improvement:
We believe that education is a continuous process of improvement. At NLP Engineering Academy, we are committed to staying up-to-date with the latest developments in AI NLP Prompt Engineering and incorporating them into our coursework. We also seek feedback from our students and faculty members to continually improve our programs and services.

Adaptive Learning:
We believe that every student learns differently. At NLP Engineering Academy, we offer adaptive learning methods that cater to individual learning styles and needs. Our coursework is designed to be accessible and engaging for all students, regardless of their background or level of experience in AI NLP Prompt Engineering.

The NLP Engineering Academy teaching philosophy and methods are designed to provide students with a comprehensive and engaging education in AI NLP Prompt Engineering. With active learning, experienced faculty, technology-driven instruction, and a student-centered approach, students can expect to gain the skills and expertise needed to succeed in this exciting and rapidly growing field.

Examples of The Types of Projects and Assignments Students Will Complete During Their Studies.

At NLP Engineering Academy, we believe in providing students with hands-on experience in AI NLP Prompt Engineering through a variety of projects and assignments. Here are some examples of the types of projects and assignments that students may expect to complete during their studies:

Capstone Projects:
Capstone projects are a key component of our degree programs in AI NLP Prompt Engineering. These projects provide students with the opportunity to apply their knowledge and skills to real-world problems. Capstone projects typically involve working on a team with other students to design, develop, and implement an AI NLP Prompt Engineering solution for a real-world client or organization.

Research Papers:

Research papers are a common assignment in our degree programs. These papers require students to conduct in-depth research on a particular topic related to AI NLP Prompt Engineering and to present their findings in a well-written and well-researched paper. Research papers provide students with an opportunity to explore topics of interest in greater depth and to develop their research and writing skills.

Programming Assignments:

Programming assignments are a critical component of our degree programs in AI NLP Prompt Engineering. These assignments require students to apply their knowledge of programming languages and tools to develop AI NLP Prompt Engineering solutions. Programming assignments typically involve working on a specific problem or task and using programming languages such as Python, Java, or C++ to develop a solution.

Group Projects:
Group projects are a common assignment in our degree programs. These projects require students to work together in groups to design, develop, and implement AI NLP Prompt Engineering solutions. Group projects provide students with an opportunity to collaborate with peers, develop teamwork skills, and gain experience in project management and coordination.

Case Studies:
Case studies are a valuable tool for learning about AI NLP Prompt Engineering in real-world contexts. These assignments require students to analyze and evaluate real-world examples of AI NLP Prompt Engineering solutions, and to present their findings in a well-written and well-researched paper or presentation. Case studies provide students with an opportunity to apply their knowledge to real-world scenarios and to develop critical thinking skills.

At NLP Engineering Academy, we provide students with the opportunity to experience a variety of projects and assignments that allow them to gain hands-on experience in AI NLP Prompt Engineering. These projects and assignments provide students with the opportunity to apply their knowledge to real-world problems, collaborate with peers, develop critical thinking and problem-solving skills, and gain experience in project management and coordination.

VI.   The Power of Networking: Building Connections and Finding Opportunities

Networking is a critical component of career success in any field, and AI NLP Prompt Engineering is no exception. At NLP Engineering Academy, we understand the importance of networking and provide students with a variety of opportunities to connect with peers, faculty members, alumni, and industry professionals. Here is an overview of the power of networking with the NLP Engineering Academy:

Alumni Network:
Our alumni network is a valuable resource for students and graduates of NLP Engineering Academy. Our alumni are successful professionals in the field of AI NLP Prompt Engineering, and they provide a wealth of knowledge and experience that can help students and graduates to succeed in their careers. Our alumni network provides opportunities for students and graduates to

connect with each other, share experiences and knowledge, and access job opportunities.

Industry Connections:
At NLP Engineering Academy, we have strong connections with industry leaders and organizations in the field of AI NLP Prompt Engineering. Our faculty members and staff members have extensive experience working in the field and can provide students with valuable connections and insights into the industry. We also offer networking events, job fairs, and other opportunities for students to connect with industry professionals and learn about job opportunities.

Peer Networking:
Networking with peers is also an important component of career success. At NLP Engineering Academy, we encourage students to connect with each other and collaborate on projects and assignments. Our online learning platform offers discussion boards, chat rooms, and other tools that allow students to connect with each other and build a sense of community. By networking with

peers, students can gain valuable insights, develop teamwork skills, and build a network of like-minded professionals.

Career Services:
At NLP Engineering Academy, we offer a range of career services to help students and graduates succeed in their careers. Our career services include resume reviews, interview coaching, and job search assistance. We also offer career development workshops and other resources that help students and graduates build their professional networks and find job opportunities.

The power of networking with the NLP Engineering Academy is an essential component of career success in AI NLP Prompt Engineering. By building connections with alumni, industry professionals, peers, and faculty members, students and graduates can gain valuable insights, access job opportunities, and build a network of support and resources that can help them succeed in their careers.

Explanation of The Importance of Networking in The Field of AI NLP Prompt Engineering

Networking is a critical component of success in the field of AI NLP Prompt Engineering. Here are some reasons why networking is important in this field:

Access to Job Opportunities:
Networking provides access to job opportunities that may not be advertised publicly. By connecting with industry professionals, attending networking events, and building relationships with peers and alumni, individuals in the field of AI NLP Prompt Engineering can learn about job openings and career opportunities that they may not have discovered otherwise.

Industry Insights:
Networking provides access to valuable industry insights and knowledge. By connecting with peers, faculty members, and industry professionals, individuals can gain

insights into the latest trends and developments in AI NLP Prompt Engineering. This knowledge can be critical to career success in this rapidly evolving field.

Professional Development:
Networking provides opportunities for professional development. By connecting with mentors and industry professionals, individuals can gain insights into career paths and strategies for career advancement. Networking events and workshops can also provide valuable opportunities for skill-building and professional development.

Collaboration and Partnership:
Networking provides opportunities for collaboration and partnership. By connecting with peers and industry professionals, individuals can find potential collaborators for research projects, startups, and other initiatives. Collaboration and partnership can be critical to success in AI NLP Prompt Engineering, where innovation and creativity are essential components of success.

Building Relationships:
Networking provides opportunities for building relationships with peers, alumni, and industry professionals. Building strong relationships is essential to success in any field, and AI NLP Prompt Engineering is no exception. Strong relationships can lead to mentorship, job opportunities, and long-term professional success.

Staying Up to Date with the Latest Trends:
Networking provides opportunities to stay up to date with the latest trends in AI NLP Prompt Engineering. By attending conferences, workshops, and other networking events, individuals can learn about the latest research and development in the field. This knowledge can be critical to staying competitive in a rapidly evolving industry.

Access to Funding:
Networking can provide access to funding opportunities for research projects, startups, and other initiatives. By connecting with

investors, grant makers, and other sources of funding, individuals can secure the resources they need to pursue their goals and make an impact in the field of AI NLP Prompt Engineering.

Developing Soft Skills:
Networking provides opportunities to develop soft skills, such as communication, teamwork, and leadership. By connecting with peers, alumni, and industry professionals, individuals can learn from different perspectives and develop their social skills. These skills are essential to success in any field, and particularly important in the collaborative, interdisciplinary field of AI NLP Prompt Engineering.

Building a Professional Brand:
Networking provides opportunities to build a professional brand and reputation. By connecting with industry professionals, individuals can build a reputation as an expert in the field and can establish a strong

online presence through social media and other digital channels. A strong professional brand can lead to job opportunities, collaboration opportunities, and other benefits.

Mentorship:
Networking provides opportunities for mentorship, which can be critical to career success. By connecting with experienced professionals in the field, individuals can learn from their experiences, gain insights into career paths, and receive guidance and support. Mentorship can be particularly valuable for individuals who are just starting their careers in AI NLP Prompt Engineering.

Networking is essential to success in the field of AI NLP Prompt Engineering. By building strong relationships, gaining industry insights, accessing job opportunities, and collaborating with peers and industry professionals, individuals in this field can achieve their career goals and make a positive impact on the industry.

Discussion of the opportunities available to NLP Prompting Academy students and alumni

At NLP Engineering Academy, we are committed to providing our students and alumni with opportunities for success in the field of AI NLP Prompt Engineering. Here are some of the opportunities available to NLP Engineering Academy students and alumni:

Internships:
NLP Engineering Academy works closely with industry leaders and organizations to provide our students with internship opportunities. These internships provide students with hands-on experience in AI NLP Prompt Engineering and can lead to job opportunities after graduation. We also provide resources and support to help students secure internships that align with their interests and career goals.

Career Services:

NLP Engineering Academy offers a range of career services to help students and alumni succeed in their careers. Our career services include resume reviews, interview coaching, and job search assistance. We also offer career development workshops and other resources that help students and graduates build their professional networks and find job opportunities.

Industry Connections:

At NLP Engineering Academy, we have strong connections with industry leaders and organizations in the field of AI NLP Prompt Engineering. Our faculty members and staff members have extensive experience working in the field and can provide students and alumni with valuable connections and insights into the industry. We also offer networking events, job fairs, and other opportunities for students to connect with industry professionals and learn about job opportunities.

Research Opportunities:
NLP Engineering Academy offers research opportunities to students who are interested in pursuing research in AI NLP Prompt Engineering. Our faculty members are engaged in cutting-edge research in the field, and students have the opportunity to work on research projects under their guidance.

Alumni Network:
Our alumni network is a valuable resource for students and graduates of NLP Engineering Academy. Our alumni are successful professionals in the field of AI NLP Prompt Engineering, and they provide a wealth of knowledge and experience that can help students and graduates to succeed in their careers. Our alumni network provides opportunities for students and graduates to connect with each other, share experiences and knowledge, and access job opportunities.

Entrepreneurship:
NLP Engineering Academy supports entrepreneurship and provides resources for students and alumni who are interested in

starting their own businesses. We offer workshops and mentoring services to help individuals develop their business plans and navigate the process of starting a business in AI NLP Prompt Engineering.

Continuing Education:
NLP Engineering Academy offers continuing education opportunities to our alumni. These opportunities allow alumni to stay up to date with the latest trends and developments in AI NLP Prompt Engineering and can lead to career advancement and new job opportunities.

Conferences and Events:
NLP Engineering Academy hosts conferences and events that bring together industry leaders and experts in the field of AI NLP Prompt Engineering. These events provide opportunities for students and alumni to learn about the latest research, trends, and best practices in the field. They also provide opportunities for networking and building relationships with other professionals in the industry.

Professional Organizations:
NLP Engineering Academy encourages students and alumni to become involved in professional organizations in the field of AI NLP Prompt Engineering. These organizations provide opportunities for networking, career development, and continuing education. They also provide a platform for individuals to share their knowledge and expertise with others in the field.

Collaboration Opportunities:
NLP Engineering Academy provides opportunities for collaboration among students, alumni, faculty members, and industry professionals. These collaborations can lead to innovative research projects, startups, and other initiatives that make a positive impact on the field of AI NLP Prompt Engineering.

The NLP Engineering Academy provides students and alumni with a range of opportunities for success in the field of AI

NLP Prompt Engineering. These opportunities include internships, career services, industry connections, research opportunities, and access to our alumni network. By taking advantage of these opportunities, students and alumni can gain valuable experience, build their professional networks, and achieve their career goals in AI NLP Prompt Engineering.

VII. Real-World Applications of AI NLP Prompt Engineering: How NLP Engineering Academy Graduates are Making a Difference

At NLP Engineering Academy, we are committed to preparing our graduates for success in the field of AI NLP Prompt Engineering. Our graduates are making a difference in the real world by applying their skills and knowledge to a range of industries and applications. Here are some examples of the real-world applications of AI NLP Prompt Engineering and how NLP Engineering Academy graduates are making a difference:

Healthcare:

NLP Engineering Academy graduates are applying their skills to healthcare applications, such as developing predictive models for disease diagnosis and treatment. By analyzing large datasets of medical records and other health data, NLP Engineering Academy graduates are developing tools and technologies that can improve patient outcomes and reduce healthcare costs.

Finance:

NLP Engineering Academy graduates are using AI NLP Prompt Engineering to analyze financial data and develop predictive models for investment and risk management. By applying machine learning algorithms to large datasets of financial data, NLP Engineering Academy graduates are helping financial institutions to make better investment decisions and manage risk more effectively.

Marketing:

NLP Engineering Academy graduates are using AI NLP Prompt Engineering to develop personalized marketing strategies and improve customer engagement. By analyzing customer data and social media interactions, NLP Engineering Academy graduates are developing marketing campaigns that are more targeted and effective.

Customer Service:

NLP Engineering Academy graduates are using AI NLP Prompt Engineering to develop chatbots and virtual assistants that can provide personalized customer service. By applying natural language processing algorithms to customer data, NLP Engineering Academy graduates are developing tools and technologies that can improve customer satisfaction and reduce customer service costs.

Education:

NLP Engineering Academy graduates are using AI NLP Prompt Engineering to develop educational technologies that can personalize learning and improve student outcomes. By analyzing student data and using machine learning algorithms, NLP Engineering Academy graduates are developing tools that can identify individual learning needs and provide customized support.

Legal:

NLP Engineering Academy graduates are applying AI NLP Prompt Engineering to the legal field, by developing tools that can automate legal research and analysis. By analyzing large datasets of legal information, NLP Engineering Academy graduates are developing technologies that can streamline legal processes, reduce costs, and improve access to justice.

Security:

NLP Engineering Academy graduates are using AI NLP Prompt Engineering to develop security applications, such as threat detection and prevention tools. By analyzing large datasets of security data and using machine learning algorithms, NLP Engineering Academy graduates are developing tools that can identify and prevent security threats in real time.

Transportation:

NLP Engineering Academy graduates are using AI NLP Prompt Engineering to develop transportation technologies, such as autonomous vehicles and traffic optimization tools. By analyzing traffic data and using machine learning algorithms, NLP Engineering Academy graduates are developing technologies that can improve safety, reduce traffic congestion, and reduce environmental impact.

Media and Entertainment:

NLP Engineering Academy graduates are using AI NLP Prompt Engineering to develop media and entertainment applications, such as personalized content recommendations and content creation tools. By analyzing user data and using machine learning algorithms, NLP Engineering

Academy graduates are developing tools that can enhance the user experience and drive engagement.

Environmental Science:

NLP Engineering Academy graduates are using AI NLP Prompt Engineering to develop environmental applications, such as climate modeling and natural disaster prediction tools. By analyzing large datasets of environmental data and using machine learning algorithms, NLP Engineering Academy graduates are developing tools that can improve our understanding of the natural world and help us to mitigate the effects of climate change.

The NLP Engineering Academy graduates are making a difference in the real world by applying their skills and knowledge to a range of industries and applications. From healthcare and finance to marketing and education, NLP Engineering Academy graduates are using AI NLP Prompt Engineering to develop innovative solutions that improve outcomes and drive progress in their respective fields.

Profiles of NLP Engineering Academy Graduates and Their Career Paths

At NLP Engineering Academy, we are proud of our graduates and their achievements in the field of AI NLP Prompt Engineering. Our graduates have gone on to pursue successful careers in a wide range of industries and applications. Here are some profiles of NLP Engineering Academy graduates and their career paths:

Profile 1 - John:

John graduated from NLP Engineering Academy with a Prompt Master's degree and went on to work for a healthcare technology company. As a data scientist, John was responsible for developing predictive models for disease diagnosis and treatment. He used AI NLP Prompt Engineering to analyze large datasets of medical records and other health data, and his work resulted in improved patient outcomes and reduced healthcare costs.

Profile 2 - Maria:

Maria graduated from NLP Engineering Academy with a Prompt Doctorate degree and went on to start her own AI NLP Prompt Engineering consulting firm. Her firm specializes in developing customized AI solutions for a range of industries, including finance, marketing, and transportation. Maria's work has been recognized for its innovation and impact, and her firm has won several awards for its contributions to the field of AI NLP Prompt Engineering.

Profile 3 - David:

David graduated from NLP Engineering Academy with a Prompt Practitioner degree and went on to work for a customer service technology company. As a software engineer,

David was responsible for developing chatbots and virtual assistants that could provide personalized customer service. He used AI NLP Prompt Engineering to analyze customer data and social media interactions, and his work resulted in improved customer satisfaction and reduced customer service costs.

Profile 4 - Sarah:

Sarah graduated from NLP Engineering Academy with a Prompt Engineer degree and went on to work for a media and entertainment company. As a machine learning engineer, Sarah was responsible for developing personalized content recommendations and content creation tools. She used AI NLP Prompt Engineering to analyze user data and machine learning algorithms to improve the user experience and drive engagement.

The NLP Engineering Academy graduates have pursued successful careers in a wide range of industries and applications, from healthcare and finance to marketing and transportation. They have used AI NLP Prompt Engineering to develop innovative solutions that improve outcomes and drive progress in their respective fields. Our graduates are making a positive impact on the world by applying their skills and knowledge of AI NLP Prompt Engineering to solve real-world problems and create new opportunities while commanding salaries from $70,000 to $300,000 per year.

Examples of How Their Education Has Prepared Them to Tackle Real-World Challenges

At NLP Engineering Academy, we are dedicated to preparing our students for success in the real world. Our rigorous curriculum and hands-on learning experiences provide students with the skills and knowledge they need to tackle real-world challenges in a variety of industries and applications. Here are some examples of how NLP Engineering Academy graduates have used their education to tackle real-world challenges:

Project-Based Learning:

NLP Engineering Academy's project-based learning approach provides students with opportunities to work on real-world projects and challenges. For example, students have worked on projects such as developing a predictive model for disease diagnosis and treatment and building a personalized content recommendation engine for a marketing company. By working on these types of projects, students develop the skills and knowledge they need to tackle real-world challenges in their future careers.

Hands-On Experience:

NLP Engineering Academy provides students with hands-on experience through internships, co-op programs, and industry partnerships. For example, students have worked as interns at companies such as Google and IBM, where they have had the opportunity to work on real-world AI NLP Prompt Engineering projects and gain practical experience in the field.

Industry-Relevant Curriculum:

NLP Engineering Academy's curriculum is designed to be relevant and up to date with the latest developments in the field of AI NLP Prompt Engineering. For example, students learn about cutting-edge technologies such as deep learning and natural language processing, which are highly relevant to the current industry landscape. By learning about these technologies, students are prepared to tackle real-world challenges in a variety of industries and applications.

Collaboration:

NLP Engineering Academy fosters collaboration among faculty members, students, and industry partners to drive innovation in the field of AI NLP Prompt Engineering. By working together on projects and challenges, students develop important collaboration and communication skills that are highly valued in the industry. This collaboration also helps to ensure that students are prepared to tackle real-world challenges in a team-oriented environment.

Mentorship:

NLP Engineering Academy provides students with mentorship opportunities through its faculty members and industry partners. Students have the opportunity to work closely with experienced professionals in the field of AI NLP Prompt Engineering, who can provide guidance and support as they tackle real-world challenges. This mentorship helps students to develop important professional skills, such as communication and problem-solving, that are essential for success in the industry.

Specialization:

NLP Engineering Academy offers students the opportunity to specialize in a particular area of AI NLP Prompt Engineering, such as natural language processing or computer vision. By specializing in a particular area, students develop a deeper understanding of the field and are better equipped to tackle real-world challenges in that area.

Entrepreneurship:

NLP Engineering Academy encourages students to develop an entrepreneurial mindset and to use their education to create new opportunities in the industry. For example, students have the opportunity to participate in entrepreneurship programs and to develop their own AI NLP Prompt Engineering startups. By developing an entrepreneurial mindset, students are prepared to tackle real-world challenges in a creative and innovative way.

Continuous Learning:

NLP Engineering Academy emphasizes the importance of continuous learning in the field of AI NLP Prompt Engineering. Graduates are equipped with the skills and knowledge they need to stay up to date with the latest developments in the field and to continue to tackle real-world challenges throughout their careers. This emphasis on continuous learning helps graduates to stay competitive in the industry and to make a real-world impact.

The NLP Engineering Academy prepares students to tackle real-world challenges in a variety of industries and applications through project-based learning, hands-on experience, industry-relevant curriculum, and collaboration. Our graduates are equipped with the skills and knowledge they need to make a real-world impact in their future careers.

VIII. The Future of AI NLP Prompt Engineering: Where We're Headed

The applications of AI NLP Prompt Engineering are virtually limitless, and we are just beginning to scratch the surface of what is possible. Here are some of the key trends and developments that are shaping the future of AI NLP Prompt Engineering:

Increased Integration with Other Technologies:

AI NLP Prompt Engineering is increasingly being integrated with other technologies, such as robotics and machine vision, to create more powerful and versatile systems. For example, AI NLP Prompt Engineering can be used to analyze text and speech data, while machine vision can be used to analyze visual data. By combining these technologies, we can create systems that are better able to understand and interact with the world around them.

Continued Development of Natural Language Processing:

Natural language processing (NLP) is a key area of AI NLP Prompt Engineering, and it is expected to continue to develop rapidly in the coming years. NLP has many applications, such as chatbots and virtual assistants, and as the technology improves, these applications will become even more sophisticated and useful.

Expansion of AI NLP Prompt Engineering into New Industries:

AI NLP Prompt Engineering is already being used in a wide range of industries, but we can expect to see even more expansion in the coming years. For example, AI NLP Prompt Engineering can be used in healthcare to analyze patient data and develop personalized treatment plans, or in finance to analyze market data and make investment decisions.

Increased Emphasis on Ethics and Privacy:

As AI NLP Prompt Engineering becomes more widespread, there is a growing concern about the ethical and privacy implications of the technology. In the coming years, we can expect to see increased emphasis on ensuring that AI NLP Prompt Engineering is used in an ethical and responsible way, and that user privacy is protected.

Advancements in Deep Learning:

Deep learning is a subset of machine learning that involves training artificial neural networks to recognize patterns in data. Deep learning has already had a major impact on the field of AI NLP Prompt Engineering, but we can expect to see even more advancements in the coming years. For example, researchers are working on developing more efficient deep learning algorithms that can handle larger datasets and more complex tasks.

Improved Human-Machine Interaction:

As AI NLP Prompt Engineering becomes more advanced, it will be important to develop better ways for humans to interact with machines. This could include things like more intuitive user interfaces, or more sophisticated chatbots and virtual assistants that can understand and respond to human emotions.

Increased Focus on Explainability:

One challenge with AI NLP Prompt Engineering is that it can be difficult to understand how a particular decision was made. As the technology becomes more widespread, there will be a growing need for explainability, or the ability to understand and explain how AI NLP Prompt Engineering systems arrive at their conclusions.

Emphasis on Data Privacy and Security:

As AI NLP Prompt Engineering becomes more widespread, there will be a growing need to ensure that data is collected, stored, and used in a responsible and secure way. This will involve developing new technologies and protocols for data privacy and security, as well as educating professionals in the field on best practices.

Collaboration between Humans and Machines:

Finally, we can expect to see increased collaboration between humans and machines in the coming years. Rather than simply replacing humans with machines, AI NLP Prompt Engineering will be used to augment human capabilities and to work together with humans to solve complex problems.

The future of AI NLP Prompt Engineering is bright, with many exciting developments on the horizon. From increased integration with other technologies to the expansion of AI

NLP Prompt Engineering into new industries, there are many opportunities for professionals in the field to make a real-world impact. As the technology continues to evolve, it will be important to keep a close eye on ethical and privacy considerations, and to ensure that AI NLP Prompt Engineering is used in a responsible and beneficial way.

Predictions for the Future of AI NLP Prompt Engineering and the Role NLP Prompting Academy Will Play in Shaping It

The future of the field is bright, and NLP Engineering Academy will play a critical role in shaping it. Here are some predictions for the future of AI NLP Prompt Engineering and the role that NLP Engineering Academy will play:

Increased Demand for AI NLP Prompt Engineering Professionals:

As the applications of AI NLP Prompt Engineering continue to expand, there will be an increasing demand for professionals with the skills and knowledge to develop and implement these technologies. NLP Engineering Academy will play a key role in meeting this demand by providing high-quality education and training to the next generation of AI NLP Prompt Engineering professionals.

Continued Advancements in Natural Language Processing:

Natural language processing is a key area of AI NLP Prompt Engineering, and it is expected to continue to advance rapidly in the coming years. NLP Engineering Academy will play a critical role in shaping these advancements by providing cutting-edge research and development in the field.

Greater Emphasis on Explainability and Transparency:

As AI NLP Prompt Engineering becomes more widespread, there will be a growing need for explainability and transparency. NLP Engineering Academy will play a key role in developing new technologies and protocols for explainability and transparency, and in educating professionals in the field on best practices.

Greater Collaboration between Industry and Academia:

As the applications of AI NLP Prompt Engineering continue to expand, there will be a growing need for collaboration between industry and academia. NLP Engineering Academy will play a critical role in fostering this collaboration by partnering with industry leaders and developing real-world applications of AI NLP Prompt Engineering technologies.

Increased Focus on Ethics and Responsible Use:

As AI NLP Prompt Engineering continues to evolve, there will be a growing need for responsible and ethical use of these technologies. NLP Engineering Academy will play a key role in educating professionals in the field on the ethical implications of AI NLP Prompt Engineering, and in developing technologies that are designed to benefit society as a whole.

Greater Integration with Other Technologies:

AI NLP Prompt Engineering will continue to be integrated with other technologies, such as robotics, IoT, and blockchain, to create more powerful and versatile systems. NLP Engineering Academy will play a critical role in developing the expertise and knowledge needed to work with these technologies and create integrated solutions.

Increased Use in Healthcare and Life Sciences:

AI NLP Prompt Engineering has many applications in healthcare and life sciences, such as analyzing medical data and developing personalized treatment plans. As these industries continue to embrace AI NLP Prompt Engineering, there will be an increasing demand for professionals with the skills and knowledge to work in these fields. NLP Engineering Academy will play a key role in meeting this demand by offering specialized coursework and training in healthcare and life sciences.

Greater Focus on User Experience:

As AI NLP Prompt Engineering becomes more prevalent in consumer-facing applications, there will be an increased focus on user experience. NLP Engineering Academy will play a critical role in developing the skills and knowledge needed to create user-friendly interfaces and applications that are accessible to a wide range of users.

Expansion into Developing Countries:

As AI NLP Prompt Engineering continues to expand globally, there will be a growing need for education and training in developing countries. NLP Engineering Academy will play a critical role in meeting this need by offering online coursework and training that is accessible from anywhere in the world.

The future of AI NLP Prompt Engineering is full of exciting possibilities, and NLP Engineering Academy will play a critical role in shaping it. By providing high-quality education and training to the next generation of AI NLP Prompt Engineering professionals, conducting cutting-edge research and development, and fostering collaboration between industry and academia, NLP Engineering Academy is well positioned to be a leader in the field for years to come.

Discussion of The School's Research and Innovation in The Field

As an expert in AI NLP Prompt Engineering education, I can attest to the importance of research and innovation in this field, and NLP Engineering Academy is at the forefront of this effort. Here is a discussion of the school's research and innovation in the field:

Cutting-edge Research:

NLP Engineering Academy is dedicated to conducting cutting-edge research in the field of AI NLP Prompt Engineering. The school's faculty and researchers are involved in a wide range of research projects, including natural language understanding, sentiment analysis, machine translation, and more. This research is essential for advancing the state of the art in AI NLP Prompt Engineering and creating new applications and use cases.

Industry Partnerships:

NLP Engineering Academy partners with leading companies and organizations in the field of AI NLP Prompt Engineering to develop real-world applications and solutions. These partnerships are essential for ensuring that the school's research and innovation efforts are aligned with the needs of the industry and that graduates are prepared to work in the field.

Innovation in Curriculum:

NLP Engineering Academy is committed to developing innovative coursework and curricula that are designed to prepare students for the challenges of the future. The school's faculty is constantly updating and refining the coursework to ensure that it is up to date with the latest developments in the field and that students are equipped with the skills and knowledge they need to succeed.

Student Research Projects:

NLP Engineering Academy encourages students to engage in research and innovation through independent research projects and capstone projects. These projects allow students to apply the skills and knowledge they have learned in coursework to real-world problems and to develop their own research interests and areas of expertise.

Publications and Presentations:

NLP Engineering Academy faculty and researchers regularly publish papers and present at conferences in the field of AI NLP Prompt Engineering. This work helps to advance the state of the art in the field, and it also helps to promote the school and its reputation as a leader in AI NLP Prompt Engineering education.

Focus on Ethical and Responsible AI:

NLP Engineering Academy is dedicated to promoting ethical and responsible use of AI NLP Prompt Engineering technologies. As such, the school's research and innovation efforts focus on developing AI NLP Prompt Engineering technologies that are designed to benefit society as a whole. This includes developing technologies that are transparent, accountable, and respectful of privacy.

Interdisciplinary Research:

NLP Engineering Academy recognizes the importance of interdisciplinary research in AI NLP Prompt Engineering. As such, the school's research and innovation efforts often involve collaboration with experts from other fields, such as psychology, linguistics, and computer science. This interdisciplinary approach helps to ensure that the school's research is well-rounded and informed by a variety of perspectives.

Collaboration with Other Institutions:

NLP Engineering Academy is committed to collaborating with other institutions in the field of AI NLP Prompt Engineering to advance the state of the art and to promote the responsible use of AI NLP Prompt

Engineering technologies. These collaborations may involve joint research projects, sharing of resources and expertise, and co-development of educational programs.

Investment in Emerging Technologies:

NLP Engineering Academy is dedicated to staying ahead of the curve in the rapidly evolving field of AI NLP Prompt Engineering. As such, the school invests in emerging technologies that are likely to have a significant impact on the field in the future. This includes technologies such as quantum computing, augmented reality, and natural language generation

The NLP Engineering Academy is committed to conducting cutting-edge research and innovation in the field of AI NLP Prompt Engineering. Through partnerships with industry leaders, innovative coursework and curricula, student research projects, and publications and presentations, the school is helping to shape the future of the field and to prepare the next generation of AI NLP Prompt Engineering professionals.

IX. Taking the Next Step: Enrolling in NLP Engineering Academy

Enrolling in NLP Engineering Academy is a smart and strategic next step for anyone interested in pursuing a career in this field. Here are some reasons why:

Comprehensive Curriculum:

NLP Engineering Academy's degree programs offer a comprehensive curriculum that covers all aspects of AI NLP Prompt Engineering, from fundamental principles to advanced applications. The coursework is designed to provide students with the skills and knowledge they need to succeed in the field, including programming languages, algorithms, data structures, and more.

World-Class Faculty:

NLP Engineering Academy's faculty is made up of experienced professionals and experts in the field of AI NLP Prompt Engineering. They are dedicated to providing high-quality education and mentorship to students, and they bring a wealth of real-world experience to the classroom.

Flexibility and Convenience:

NLP Engineering Academy's degree programs are offered online, which makes them highly flexible and convenient for students. This means that students can study at their own pace and on their own schedule, without having to uproot their lives or disrupt their work or family obligations.

Career Support:

NLP Engineering Academy is committed to helping students achieve their career goals in the field of AI NLP Prompt Engineering. The school provides career support services, including job search assistance, networking opportunities, and access to industry experts and employers.

Competitive Salaries:

As we've discussed, the demand for AI NLP Prompt Engineering professionals is rapidly increasing, and salaries in the field are highly competitive. By obtaining a degree from NLP Engineering Academy, students can position themselves for lucrative and rewarding careers in this exciting field.

State-of-the-Art Technology:

NLP Engineering Academy invests in state-of-the-art technology and resources to provide students with the best possible learning experience. The school uses cutting-edge software and tools to simulate real-world scenarios and projects, providing students with hands-on experience in a safe and controlled environment.

Diversity and Inclusion:

NLP Engineering Academy is committed to promoting diversity and inclusion in the field of AI NLP Prompt Engineering. The school strives to create an environment that is welcoming and supportive of all students, regardless of their background or identity. This diversity of perspectives and experiences enhances the learning environment and prepares students to work effectively in a global and diverse workplace.

Alumni Network:

NLP Engineering Academy has a strong and active alumni network, which provides students with valuable networking opportunities and connections to professionals in the field. Alumni are often involved in hiring decisions and can provide guidance and mentorship to current students, helping them to achieve their career goals.

Lifelong Learning:

NLP Engineering Academy recognizes that AI NLP Prompt Engineering is a rapidly evolving field, and that professionals must continually update their skills and knowledge to remain competitive. The school offers lifelong learning opportunities, including continuing education courses and professional development workshops, to help alumni and other professionals stay up to date with the latest trends and technologies.

Enrolling in NLP Engineering Academy is an excellent next step for anyone interested in pursuing a career in AI NLP Prompt Engineering. With a comprehensive curriculum, world-class faculty, flexibility and convenience, career support, and competitive salaries, NLP Engineering Academy offers everything students need to succeed in this rapidly growing field.

Step-By-Step Guide to The Application Process and Enrollment

A step-by-step guide to the online application process and enrollment at NLP Engineering Academy. Here are the steps:

Choose a Degree Program:

NLP Engineering Academy offers four degree programs in AI NLP Prompt Engineering: Prompt Practitioner, Prompt Engineer, Prompt Master, and Prompt Doctor. Review the program requirements and choose the degree program that best fits your career goals.

Complete the Online Application:

Visit the NLP Engineering Academy website and complete the online application form.

You will need to provide personal and academic information, including transcripts and test scores. There may be an application fee, which varies by program.

Submit Supporting Materials:

In addition to the online application, you may need to submit supporting materials, such as letters of recommendation, a personal statement, or a resume. Be sure to check the specific requirements for your chosen degree program.

Await Notification:

After submitting your application and supporting materials, you will receive notification of your admission status. If you are admitted, you will receive information on how to enroll in your chosen degree program.

Enroll in Classes:

Once you are admitted, you can enroll in classes for your chosen degree program. NLP Engineering Academy offers online classes that are flexible and convenient for students. You will work with an academic advisor to develop a course plan that meets your academic and career goals.

Receive Grants and Scholarships:

NLP Engineering Academy offers a variety of grants and scholarships to help students cover the cost of their education. You can apply for financial aid by completing the Free Application for Federal Student Aid (FAFSA). In addition, NLP Engineering Academy offers scholarships to students who demonstrate academic achievement, financial need, or other criteria.

The online application process and enrollment at NLP Engineering Academy is straightforward and user-friendly. By following these steps and applying for grants and scholarships, students can take advantage of the many benefits of an AI NLP Prompt Engineering education, including a comprehensive curriculum, world-class faculty, flexible scheduling, and career support.

Information on Tuition, Scholarships, and Financial Aid Options

As an expert in AI NLP Prompt Engineering education, I can provide information on tuition, scholarships, and financial aid options available at NLP Engineering Academy.

Tuition:

NLP Engineering Academy's tuition varies depending on the degree program and the number of courses taken per semester. On average, tuition is approximately $10,000 per course. However, the cost may be higher or lower depending on the specific program and course load.

Scholarships:

NLP Engineering Academy offers a variety of scholarships to help students cover the cost of their education. These scholarships may be based on academic merit, financial need, or other criteria. For example, NLP Engineering Academy offers scholarships of up to $9,500 for qualified students, veterans, and workers obtaining upskills to stay current with technology.

Financial Aid:

In addition to scholarships, NLP Engineering Academy offers financial aid in the form of grants, loans, and work-study programs. To be eligible for financial aid, students must complete the Free Application for Federal Student Aid (FAFSA) and meet certain eligibility requirements. NLP Engineering Academy's financial aid office can assist students in navigating the application process and identifying the best options for their individual needs.

Other Funding Options:

NLP Engineering Academy also encourages students to explore other funding options, such as employer tuition reimbursement programs or private scholarships. These options may provide additional financial support for students pursuing an AI NLP Prompt Engineering degree.

The NLP Engineering Academy offers a range of tuition, scholarship, and financial aid options to help students finance their education. With scholarships of up to $9,500 for qualified students, veterans, and workers obtaining upskills to stay current with technology, NLP Engineering Academy is committed to making AI NLP Prompt Engineering education accessible and affordable for all.

X.   DO IT: Your journey to Becoming a Prompt Engineer Starts Here

Your to DO IT: Your Journey to Becoming a Prompt Engineer Starts Here. This short marketing book is designed to provide an overview of the AI NLP Prompt Engineering field, the benefits of enrolling in the NLP Engineering Academy, and the steps you can take to start your journey as a Prompt Engineer.

In this book, you will discover:

The Growing Demand for Prompt Engineers:

AI NLP Prompt Engineering is a rapidly growing field with a high demand for skilled professionals. This book will provide you with an overview of the field and the opportunities available to those with a degree in Prompt Engineering.

The Benefits of Enrolling in the NLP Engineering Academy:

NLP Engineering Academy is a leading institution in the field of AI NLP Prompt Engineering education. In this book, you will learn about the benefits of enrolling in the school, including the comprehensive curriculum, state-of-the-art technology, and strong alumni network.

The Four Degrees of Prompt Engineering:

NLP Engineering Academy offers four-degree programs in Prompt Engineering, including Prompt Practitioner, Prompt Engineer, Prompt Master, and Prompt Doctor. This book will provide an overview of each degree program and the career prospects associated with them.

The Online Learning Experience:

NLP Engineering Academy offers online classes that are flexible and convenient for students. In this book, you will learn about the online learning experience, including the resources and support services available to students.

Funding Options:

The cost of education can be a barrier for many students. This book will provide information on scholarships, grants, and other funding options available to NLP Engineering Academy students.

Whether you are just starting your career or looking to upskill in the field of AI NLP Prompt Engineering, DO IT: Your Journey to Becoming a Prompt Engineer Starts Here is the perfect resource to help you achieve your goals. So what are you waiting for? Start reading and take the first step towards becoming a Prompt Engineer today!

Pursue a Career in AI NLP Prompt Engineering

Now is the time to pursue a career in this field. Here are some reasons why:

High Demand for Skilled Professionals:

The demand for skilled AI NLP Prompt Engineers is rapidly growing in a variety of industries. According to recent studies, there will be over 50 million jobs created in Prompt Engineering in the next five years, with salaries ranging from $70,000 to $300,000 per year for those with Prompt Degrees like those provided by NLP Engineering Academy. By pursuing a career in this field, you can enjoy excellent job security and opportunities for advancement.

Exciting and Dynamic Field:

AI NLP Prompt Engineering is an exciting and dynamic field that is constantly evolving. As a Prompt Engineer, you will have the opportunity to work on cutting-edge technologies and develop innovative solutions to complex problems. You will be at the forefront of shaping the future of technology and making a real difference in the world.

Comprehensive Curriculum:

NLP Engineering Academy offers a comprehensive curriculum in AI NLP Prompt Engineering that covers a wide range of topics, including natural language processing, machine learning, and data analysis. You will develop the skills and knowledge needed to succeed in this field and achieve your career goals.

Online Learning:

NLP Engineering Academy offers online classes that are flexible and convenient for students. This allows you to balance your education with your personal and professional obligations. With the school's online learning environment, resources, and support services, you can receive a high-quality education without having to leave your home or workplace.

Impactful Work:

AI NLP Prompt Engineering is a field that has the potential to make a significant impact on society. Prompt Engineers are developing solutions to some of the world's most pressing problems, such as healthcare, climate change, and energy efficiency. By pursuing a career in this field, you will have the opportunity to make a real difference in people's lives.

Diversity of Applications:

AI NLP Prompt Engineering has applications in a wide range of industries, from healthcare to finance to entertainment. This means that as a Prompt Engineer, you will have the opportunity to work in a field that aligns with your interests and passions.

Rapid Advancements:

AI NLP Prompt Engineering is a field that is rapidly advancing, with new technologies and innovations being developed all the time. As a Prompt Engineer, you will have the opportunity to stay at the forefront of these advancements and contribute to the development of new technologies.

Transferable Skills:

The skills that you develop as a Prompt Engineer are highly transferable, meaning that you can apply them to a variety of different industries and roles. This gives you the flexibility to explore different career paths and opportunities.

Global Opportunities:

AI NLP Prompt Engineering is a field that is in demand all over the world, meaning that there are opportunities to work internationally. This allows you to gain a diverse range of experiences and work with people from different cultures and backgrounds.

Competitive Salaries:

AI NLP Prompt Engineering is a field that offers competitive salaries, with the potential to earn a high income with the right skills and experience. Salaries for Prompt Engineers can range from $70,000 to $300,000 per year, depending on your level of education, experience, and the industry you work in.

Job Growth:

The demand for Prompt Engineers is growing rapidly, with a projected job growth rate of 21% between 2020 and 2030, according to the U.S. Bureau of Labor Statistics. This means that there will be plenty of job opportunities available for those with the right skills and qualifications.

Career Advancement:

AI NLP Prompt Engineering is a field that offers plenty of opportunities for career advancement, with the potential to move into management or executive roles. By pursuing a career in this field, you can build a rewarding and fulfilling career with plenty of opportunities for growth.

Pursuing a career now in AI NLP Prompt Engineering is an excellent choice for those who are looking for job security, exciting opportunities, and a dynamic field. With the comprehensive curriculum offered by NLP Engineering Academy and the school's online learning environment, there has never been a better time to pursue a career in this field. So why not take the first step today?